TAKE D MILK, Nah?

AN ENTRY FOR THE
Stephen   Leacock   Award
FOR HUMOUR FOR
2022

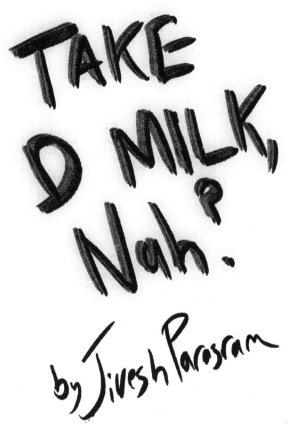

TAKE D MILK, Nah?

by Jivesh Parasram

co-created with Tom Arthur Davis
and Graham Isador

Playwrights Canada Press
Toronto

LIBRARY AND ARCHIVES CANADA CATALOGUING IN PUBLICATION
Title: Take d milk, nah? / Jivesh Parasram.
Other titles: Take the milk, nah?
Names: Parasram, Jivesh, author.
Description: A play.
Identifiers: Canadiana (print) 20210105178 | Canadiana (ebook) 20210107774 | ISBN 9780369100986 (softcover) | ISBN 9780369100993 (PDF) | ISBN 9780369101006 (HTML) | ISBN 9780369101013 (Kindle)
Classification: LCC PS8631.A7365 T35 2021 | DDC C812/.6—dc23

Playwrights Canada Press operates on Mississaugas of the Credit, Wendat, Anishinaabe, Métis, and Haudenosaunee land. It always was and always will be Indigenous land.

We acknowledge the financial support of the Canada Council for the Arts, the Ontario Arts Council (OAC), Ontario Creates, and the Government of Canada for our publishing activities.

Canada Council for the Arts   Conseil des arts du Canada

ONTARIO ARTS COUNCIL
CONSEIL DES ARTS DE L'ONTARIO
an Ontario government agency
un organisme du gouvernement de l'Ontario

Canadä

ONTARIO CREATES | ONTARIO CRÉATIF

To all those who crossed the Kala Pani.

To Mom and Dad for being my constant inspiration.

To Ajay, Amit, and Shiva for carrying me on your shoulders, knocking out a few of my teeth, and being with me till the end.

To Duke, who saved not just my life, but all of ours.

To my cousins back home for never making me feel like an outsider, despite my own baggage.

To my cousins out here, who know what I'm talking about . . .

To my uncles and aunties who I miss more than you know. Even if I don't show it.

And most of all, to Aurora and Ayaan. Who I love more than I'll ever be able to express.

So you know where we come from.

Foreword

Tom Arthur Davis and Graham Isador

GRAHAM: The first incarnation of *Take d Milk, Nah?* was created for a storytelling night I used to run. The theme I'd chosen for that month was Far From Home or Identity or something. I can't remember exactly. I always chose the themes kind of arbitrarily. I could have just as easily picked Pets or Spicy Foods. Anyways, I asked Jiv to perform on the show because Jiv is one of the funniest and brightest people I know. He's also prone to overintellectualizing. I asked for a tight five-minute story—something light and comedic—and what I got was half an hour of sprawling, witty pontification on colonialism, family, and personal history all told through the lens of birthing a cow. Even in that first draft we all recognized it was something special. Still, the night of the storytelling show I was pissed off because Jiv had gone so far over his time. Tom, you were very adamant that night that the monologue should be expanded into a play.

TOM: Yeah, but not in any way that Jiv would have approved of. I was imagining the very thing that he makes fun of in the prologue. The heartwarming journey of a young kid struggling to find his cultural identity in Canada, and then, just as he's at a crossroads in his life, travels to Trinidad and helps his family birth a cow. And in the process, I guess . . . birth his identity? I dunno. It was a bad idea. I was picturing using a giant cow puppet, and like an actor who'd play the role of all his family members. Basically it's that play you've already seen a thousand times on stages across the country. Luckily Jiv told me I was stupid (as is the typical Pandemic Theatre dramaturgical style) and we made something a bit different.

GRAHAM: The process of putting the show together pushed all of our friendships a bit. Jiv was so honest and open with his experiences. We could be kind of ruthless about what was and wasn't working. The two of you are family to me. That means we can be really open and we can also get under each other's skin. Because the two of you have read more books than I have and are generally more intelligent, I felt like it was my job to constantly ask for things to be explained as simply as they could. I also went on a lot about beginnings, middles, and ends. I think that was useful and at the same time really frustrating for Jiv. One day he pointed out that I was trying to impose a Western form onto the format of the show and, in some ways, his thoughts in general. Which at first was really maddening. I only wanted to help! But when I thought about it more . . . it kind of spoke to the bigger point of the play. What do we let shape us? What are the stories we let people tell about us? What stories do we tell about ourselves? Those answers aren't simple for Jiv. Which is probably why he couldn't just give me five minutes on that first storytelling show.

TOM: My experience was not far off from your own. Sure, I read the *Ramayana* and *The Bhagavad Gita* a few times leading into the process, but I somehow doubt my pontificating about action versus inaction for a few hours led to any great insights for Jiv, whose family runs a Hindu temple and school. So really, just like you, I was approaching this whole project from a Western, global north, colonial perspective. Because how could I not? I hope on some level that us asking all the inappropriate questions helped shape the show for Jiv. Helped him articulate what he needed to articulate to a "mainstream" audience more clearly and succinctly. But on the other hand I know how frustrating it can be to have to explain one's "marginalization," to have to educate the audience. Jiv's had to do that in his work, and his life, for a long time. And I'm sure it's both exhausting and boring. So I'm glad we managed to find a unique way for Jiv to drop that performative teaching role within the show, if even for only a few minutes.

GRAHAM: The big takeaway from that experience of making the show—and really I think why *Take d Milk* has been so successful in general—is because Jiv offers up all of this heady and raw and emotional content in a way that really lets people in. The show feels like the best conversations we have had over the years. Like, I think *Take d Milk* gave me a better understanding of race and privilege. It popped a lot of bubbles about my world view. At the same time it let me know Jiv so much better, despite the fact he's been one of my closest friends for my entire adult life. And that is wild to have happened from a piece of theatre. Even one you helped make.

When I saw the finished version I was so excited, but I felt so close to it that I had no idea if it would work. Like—spoilers—but Jiv kind of becomes a cow at one point and then we go inside his mind. I LOVE that part, but it is also really fucking weird.

TOM: That moment in the creation process was weirdly a breakthrough. At that point we had a forty-minute storytelling version of that saccharine play that I had wanted Jiv to make years before. It was funny, charming, and moving, but we were struggling to know what the action of the piece was. Not just for Jiv, but for the audience. Two of the major questions going into each new creation process at Pandemic are, what is the political action and what do we want the audience to choose?

Jiv was frustrated at the idea of staging his identity, both as a "marginalized" person and as a Hindu. There's no action for the audience if they're simply asked to "feel something." And the very idea of a "Hindu identity" is an oxymoron, because Hindus don't believe in identity. I remember being in the TPM Backspace and Jiv ranting about it and shouting about how "THIS PLAY HAS NO ACTION!" So I got him to pick up a microphone and continue his rant about identity, identity plays, and performative identity. I then asked him to start mooing like a cow for some reason. I don't remember why, but it was very funny. That's when the whole thing tilted into becoming a play about the limits of the identity play as opposed to an identity play itself.

GRAHAM: If there is anything you'd want people to get out of the written text, what would it be?

TOM: Spoilers! I'll speak to the "kicking out" of the mainstream audience section. As that's the part that everyone remembers most. And I think in many ways they misremember, because they feel fragile about the experience. And I don't mean that in a pejorative sense. I think the typical "mainstream" theatre-goer is extraordinarily well-intentioned. They go to the theatre to learn, feel, and hear new ideas. Hell, if they're coming to see a play by a dude named Jivesh Parasram, they're probably interested in learning more about a culture that is foreign to their own. On some level that is admirable. But then they get to the theatre and that same guy with the foreign name is telling them to leave because what he's about to say isn't for them. Fuck that, right?! I paid for my ticket, and I came to learn something, dammit. Who is this guy to tell me who I am anyway? He doesn't know my life.

Shortly after we premiered *Take d Milk, Nah?*, Jackie Sibblies Drury's Pulitzer Prize–winning drama *Fairview* premiered off-Broadway. Much like *Take d Milk, Nah?*, *Fairview* is noted for having a moment that speaks directly to a "marginalized audience." I don't want to misinterpret Drury's brilliant work, nor spoil anything, but I wanted to highlight this to point to the fact that artists are now starting to challenge who art is for.

For those who might feel fragile by the idea of Jiv asking you to leave the space for a brief period, I want you to reframe that anger as an opportunity for introspection. Jiv is uninterested in pointing out the white faces in the audience and telling them to scram. Actually, quite the opposite. People have multiple intersections to their identity, both visible and invisible. Instead Jiv wants you to reflect on your own life experiences and decide whether you want to stay to listen or leave to make room for those who don't often get to experience art created for them. It's that decision where the show's political action lies. Which way do you want to show your solidarity? By staying or leaving?

Tom Arthur Davis is a Toronto-based theatre artist and producer. He co-founded Pandemic Theatre in 2009, where he has created most of his work in close collaboration with Jivesh Parasram. Since 2018, Tom has acted as a producer for Why Not Theatre, where he leads the company's Provoke Activities initiatives that help remove barriers for artists. Tom's works for the stage include Mahmoud *(co-writer, Playwrights Canada Press, 2015),* Take d Milk, Nah? *(co-creator/dramaturge, Playwrights Canada Press, 2021), and* The Only Good Indian *(co-creator/co-writer).*

Graham Isador is a writer and photographer in Toronto. He is a former contributing editor at VICE. *His work has also appeared at* GQ, Men's Health, *and* The Globe and Mail. *Isador's latest play,* White Heat, *won outstanding performance text at the SummerWorks performance festival in 2019.*

A Note on Adaptation

As this is a solo show with a fair amount of autobiographical content, on first read it might seem like it's a piece that couldn't be easily taken up by another performer. I'm not sure that that's the case. On the one hand I think it could be done *as is*, so to speak, since ultimately it's the work of actors in particular to inhabit the world of a story, and I wouldn't want to limit the scope of any artist's craft of interpretation. Personally, I'm quite open to how someone might come at a process of adapting the piece, whether that means performing the text that is written here, or through inserting parts of their own experience. I believe that there are incidents (embellished and downplayed) described in the text that I'm certain are not exclusive to my experience. That said, there are certain things that I believe should remain the same.

The first is that the character's name is "Jiv." I hope it will become clear as to why this must be the case. I mention it because my name is not "Jiv"—though "Jiv" is part of my name. I wrote the piece as a character. While there's a very liminal difference between that character and myself, it is decidedly a character.

The second is that the piece should incorporate an element of ritual. The structure of the piece is built around my interpretation of yagna and puja as performed in Trinidad by Hindus in my own tradition. The symbolic actions of these rituals that are performed on stage have always been very much that—symbolic of an actual puja or yagna. And so I would be very open to interpretations truthful to the would-be performer.

In terms of further adaptation, for example, swapping out stories . . . it's certainly possible. If that's the way you'd like to go—or in fact for most forms of adaptation it would be great to have a conversation beforehand. This is less about policing what is acceptable as much as it's about ensuring that we're both on "the same page" about the intent of each story or element of ritual. The second half is probably the most difficult to change. However, this latter half draws more directly on found texts in critical race theory and puranic adaptation, so in some ways there is less "adaptation work" to be done there.

There's also a playfulness and an aspect to the performance drawing on jeu and complicité as we've come at them in our production and touring activities. As such, particularly due to the direct address nature, there's some improvisation in the moment—and things we've localized for different audiences based on the territory we're performing on. In any adaptation I'd encourage a similar principle of play and reflexiveness to the territory that you're performing on. But again, I have no interest in diminishing the importance of interpretation, and so I'm always open to another person's take. Feel free to get in touch with me if you'd like!

Jivesh Parasram,
January 2021
Unceded Algonquin Territory
(Ottawa, ON)

Take d Milk, Nah? was first performed at Pressgang Storytelling, Toronto, and further developed at b current's rock.paper.sistahz festival, Toronto; the Monsoon Festival, Surrey/Vancouver; the Caminos Festival, Toronto; and in residence with Theatre Passe Muraille, Toronto.

The play premiered at the Theatre Passe Muraille Backspace in a co-production by Pandemic Theatre and b current performing arts in association with Theatre Passe Muraille.

Performed by Jivesh Parasram
Directed by Tom Arthur Davis
Dramaturgy by Graham Isador and Tom Arthur Davis
Stage Managed by Heather Bellingham
Production and Crew Management by Christopher Ross
Set and Costume Design by Anahita Dehbonehie
Lighting Design by Rebecca Vandevelde
Sound Design by Jivesh Parasram
ASL Adaptation and Performance by Tamyka Bullen and Tala Jalili

The same production was presented by the Cultch, Vancouver, in the fall of 2019 as a touring co-production by Pandemic Theatre and Rumble Theatre in association with Neworld Theatre. It subsequently toured to the National Arts Centre, Ottawa. It was just about to open at Theatre Passe Muraille, then hit the road to Montréal, arts interculturels, Montreal, in spring 2020 as a touring co-production by Pandemic Theatre and Rumble Theatre in association with b current performing arts and Theatre Passe Muraille, however, COVID-19 had other plans. An audio version of the production was created in isolation for CBC's PlayME podcast, with significant sonic adaptation by Greg Sinclair.

*As the audience enters, there's a relatively loud pre-show playlist going. A mix of Trinidadian calypso, soca, chutney, dance hall, bhangramuffin, and classic upbeat Hindi-language cinema tunes.**

*On stage are hanging curtains in red and saffron, bringing the stage picture close to the audience. Nestled in the curtains is a small table acting as a makeshift altar, or puja table. It is covered in a bed of earth—referencing a bedi.*** On the earth there is positioned an*

---

* This can obviously change, but much of what we were working with was to create a feeling of "home"—or at least that's how people described it to us. The tunes we were using really picked up on the music we had access to growing up in the '90s—which was really a mix of Trini music with the Hindi-language cinema music (pre-Bollywood) that was essential to my parents' generation. Still it's the kind of music that seems to cross generations to a certain extent. Especially Mohammad Rafi. He was a big deal in Trinidad. Apparently when he came to visit Trinidad the first time they had to shut down the highway to the airport 'cause Indians were so into it! Another genre that is a bit less known is "bhangramuffin"—this is really led by Apache Indian, who, in the diaspora, was an amazing artist to us. He blended Caribbean "raggamuffin" style with Punjabi "bhangra" style and has had an amazing and underrated career. If you don't know him, look him up. He's exceptional.

** A retangular platform used in Carribbean rituals of worship, traditionally lined with ghobur (cow dung). Often on the surface there is a Yantra drawn of the presiding deity for the ceremony. Or, alternatively, just a rectangle with an "x" to divide the sections for a simpler ceremony. We omitted that on the table in our production.

earthen Kalsa,* a medium earthen diya,** a small brass incense burner (with pre-set incense), a small brass dish with a white teeka stick,*** a medium brass lota**** with a brass spoon holding water, and a book—the Ramcharitmanas—*wrapped in the same type of fabric that hangs around the stage.*

On the floor there is a pattern, gold on black. It's difficult to determine exactly what it is since it's bisected by the curtains.

To stage left (slightly off the pattern on the ground) there is a laptop on a stand, which the performer will use to trigger much of the sound in the show. There is also a wireless mic on a straight stand with a circular base—slightly evoking a crooner/stand-up vibe.

A light haze fills the room.

---

*   Essentially an earthen wide-mouthed pot. Traditionally it is the "centrepiece" of the ceremony as it represents all of the elements. Made of earth, filled with water and air, and often a diya is placed on top (fire).

**   An earthen lantern. Ghee or some form of oil is used as fuel with a cotton wick.

***   I actually don't know if this is the right word for this . . . It's what we call it in Trinidad, but it can be hard to find by that name in Indian puja stores. It's basically a stick you wet and use to make a marking on the forehead when performing ritual. The mark is often called a teeka or a teelka. Which spelling is correct? . . . Well, Sanskrit is all transliterated anyway. This will probably come up a lot, so go with me on this one if you know different spellings!

****   Essentially a brass pot. It looks like the Kalsa.

When ready, the pre-show playlist shifts to an intro track* for THE PERFORMER as they enter. They acknowledge the audience and they trigger a cue on the laptop, bringing the music out.

THE PERFORMER: Hi! I'm Jiv. Thanks for coming to my identity play!

So, who here knows what an identity play is?

THE PERFORMER surveys the audience to see if anyone knows.

'K. Cool!

So, for everybody else,
an identity play is a show in which the protagonist—
so the main person in the show—
they discover a conflict within *themselves.*

So maybe they've always thought they were like "X" identity,
and then they meet someone who challenges that,
and they feel something in themselves *shift.*

---

* We used "Make Way for the Indian" by Apache Indian featuring Tim Dog. Again, he's awesome. You could really use anything—but there's something about bhangramuffin music that feels right. There's also a lot of stuff that could be drawn on from chutney and soca—but it's the fusion of something distinctly "Indian" and "Caribbean" that matters. Or ya know, whatever works for you.

So ... like—Luke Skywalker!

Luke Skywalker,
he lives on Tatooine and he's basically just a moisture
farmer ...
but he knows that he wants more!
Then this droid shows up with a message from Princess
Leia: "Help me, Obi-Wan ... "

> *THE PERFORMER allows some space for the audience to
> finish the line.*

" ... you're my only hope." That's right! It's that kinda show.

So then Luke goes and he finds Obi-Wan—
and Obi-wan's like:
"Let's go, guy!"
and then Luke's like:
"Ah, nah, guy, I can't! I gotta farm all this mositure!"

So that's Luke feeling something in himself shift.

But then the Empire burns Luke's family alive—
Which is kind of ironic, because they farm moisture—
And so off he goes to fulfill his destiny as a great Jedi knight![*]

---

[*] So far, neither Disney nor Lucasfilm has sued us. I mean ... this has
gotta be fair use at this point ...

Anyway—that's the basic structure:
essentially someone is at conflict with who they truly are,
then they go on a journey and discover either their true identity,
or that they were always okay from the get-go.

Then everybody in the audience, they feel good about that person
having found their identity . . .
Maybe they remember their own identity . . .
Maybe they call their family.
The. End.

Now, a lot of people, they do an identity play
once they graduate from theatre school?
The more pretentious of us,
we wait about ten, twelve years* or so to truly "find our voice."

And if they're really pretentious assholes they do it as a solo show!

. . . And if you've never been to a solo show before—good for you!

So, basically, a solo show kinda works like this:
First, there's this part where the performer comes out,
and they're like:

---

* This changed based on how long I'd been out of theatre school. If you're doing it with another performer this should similarly be adapted to a reasonable-seeming time to them completing their training. Or if they haven't trained formally—make up some equivalent. (I *barely* trained formally).

"Oh, hey guys, what's going on? We're just talking!
The show hasn't started yet!
This is all totally off the cuff—not scripted at all!"

And then the performer, they'll tell some stories from like,
their childhood, and like puberty, and online dating,
and about their grandmother's hands.
And then at some point, they'll introduce a "nostalgic element" like:

> *THE PERFORMER goes to the computer and triggers in a
> "nostalgic" sonic element.**

Right? And then they don't really mention it for a while.
But in the middle, they'll do this monologue that's like:

> *They take centre stage and deliver the next in an overly
> indulgent, broody tone.*

"And my dad doesn't understand me!
And I just want to connect!
But my masculinity hurts!
And I think about that song ... "

> *They stare out, really "feeling" the music.*

And then there's a dramatic pause like:

---

* We used "Everybody Hurts" by R.E.M. This could be swapped out—we
just thought it was pretty funny. Whatever is used should just be consistent throughout the piece ... you'll see ... also—so far—no lawsuit!
Should be within fair use.

They play up an overly dramatic pause for a moment.
Then, checking in with the audience for a brief moment,
turn off the music.

And then, because it's a solo show, they'll do a lot of this
thing where they're like having an intense conversation with
someone—like their dad—or if we wanna get really 2010—like
their mom—but playing both parts—like:

For this next section they stand static, playing both
characters with minimal differentiation. Maybe some
vocal shift, but it's pretty half-assed. Each line shifts
between "character."

"Hi."

"Hi."

"It's been a long time."

"Yes, it has."

"Your hair is different."

"Yes."

"Did you get a haircut?"

"No."

"Oh . . ."

"Yes . . . "

"It looks different."

"I'm parting it to the
side now."

"Pardon?"

"I'm parting it to the
side now."

"Oh . . . Do you put product in it?"

"A little."

"It looks good."

"Thank you . . .
. . . Also I have cancer."

And then somebody dies,
and then they go for a walk . . .
And then through some free-form movement *experience*,
including this movement:

*They perform a "movement theatre reach."**

they see a bird or something and they say:

---

* Basically reaching to the audience. But with urgency and "meaning."
It should look pretty stupid.

THE PERFORMER rushes to the computer to trigger the "nostalgic" track.

"I know you're still with me . . .
Because I can feel you in here! . . .
And what I was looking for . . . all along . . .
was really . . . just . . . me!"

Then it snows.

They cut the track.

It's faaaackin' stupid!

And I don't know if the snowing thing is just a Canadian identity-play thing—or if all identity plays have it.
Right! And that's a thing—identity plays are especially popular in Canada.
And if not popular—common.

And I promise, we're gonna start in a sec—but I think this next part is good for context.

I think—I *think*—the reason there are so many *Canadian* identity plays is because in the 1950s and '60s there was this national commission. And this was responsible for the creation of the Canada Council for the Arts—
thanks, by the way—
and that organization had a real priority to define what *Canadian identity* was.
Ergo: funding.

But—then they mainly funded work about the settler colonial history of Canada.

And mainly English Canada.

Then French Canada, they got all pissy about it so they did their own.

Then they both realized that Indigenous people existed.

So then a bunch of white guys wrote identity plays *for* Indigenous people—'cause I guess that seemed like a good idea—
then there were people of colour just popping up out of nowhere!
There were queer people,
there were poor people,
there were people with disabilities . . .
there were women?!

. . . And I hear there's even something called . . . "women of colour."
BUT HOW!? THAT'S like two at once!!!??
Queer women of colour?!—WHAT THE FUUUUUCK?!!!?!?!?!?

As far as I can tell, this is actually the first Indo-Caribbean-Hindu-Canadian identity play ever done.
So we are making highly hyphenated history here!
And using tax dollars!

> *THE PERFORMER gives a positive "victory" gesture—
> maybe accompanied with a "yes!"*

Thing is . . . I never really wanted to do an identity play
. . . 'cause . . .
I think they're kinda wanky.
'Cause identities are intersectional,
and my experience is just my experience—
no matter how handsome a brown man I am*—
and my mom says—very handsome.

I also feel conflicted.
Because in some ways, by contributing to the "canon" of
Canadian identity plays, I'm supporting the idea that the
state of Canada is a real thing.
And I don't.**
In fact, the only thing towards territory I would like to recognize
is that this land of Tkoronto where I get to live has been the ter-
ritory of the Huron-Wendat, Haudenosaunee, the Cree, and the
Anishinaabek peoples—most recently the Mississaugas.***

---

* This is based on the original performer being and presenting as a
brown man. This could *potentially* be changed . . . though, it might shift
some of the content later on.

** Here I mean I don't recognize the idea of states as soverign bodies.
When we were at the National Arts Centre it was particularly funny for
us to add in, "Though it's great to be here at the *National* Arts Centre." I
do love me some contradiction.

*** The territorial acknowledgement should change based on where the
piece is being performed. Though I would appreciate that there be reference that the place in which the piece was created was on the territory
noted here. I'm open to different ways of acknowledging that. But the
key being that there should be an understanding of the Dish With One
Spoon wampum belt covenent that governs the territory now known
colonially as "Toronto." We often would say that it was originally created
there, and then name each nation or territory that the production had
visited, ending with the territory that we were presenting it on. Do what
feels right, but please do observe protocol in a good way.

And I say territory—and not state—because it means this is
a shared territory.
Not property that anyone owns.

So . . . all to say—didn't really want to do an identity play.
But then I did this story, about a cow I knew one time, at
my buddy Graham's storytelling night.*
And then my other buddy Tom—who I run this theatre com-
pany with**—was like:
"Dude! That should be a play!"

And I was like:
"Fuck no! There's way more interesting things to do a play
about.
What about like colonization?
Or like the dangers of nationalism?
Or like marginalization theory?"

And then Graham was like:

"Oh yeah man, that sounds awesome. Everybody wants to sit
in the dark and hear about marginalization theory."
He writes for *Vice*.

---

* This is in the context of the original production and acknowledging
my co-creators. There's likely a way to shift this around in adaptation to
a different performer.

** This is in the context of the play being produced by Pandemic Theatre.
The original production was never actually produced by any one company.
So at times I would note that Tom was who I run Pandemic Theatre with.
This would certainly be a point to consider in adaptation—again, my
intention is to acknowledge my co-creators. At this point you probably
get that things change in adaptation, so I'll stop drawing attention to it.

So yeah, I am conflicted.
Because while I think identity plays are wanky,
and I don't want to implicitly support the idea of the state
of Canada—
I also recognize that representing your identity is important.
'Cause did anyone here know that this past March marked
101 years since the end of Indian Indentureship?*

> *THE PERFORMER waits for a reaction and takes a read
> of the audience, changing their response if need be.***

And hey, it's okay if you didn't know that.
You don't hold any guilt or shame for not knowing that.
We're all *allies* here.
. . . Maybe no one ever told you.

Does anyone here know what Indian Indentureship was?

> *They wait for a reaction.*

And again. You don't need to hold any guilt or shame if you
don't know.
Maybe no one ever told you.
Because history, *mainstream* history, is like that.

---

* This date was what was used in the original production. As such,
we adjusted the date depending on when we were performing it. The
original date was based on the Indian Indentureship in Trinidad—however, by 2020 we returned to "one hundred years since the end of the
Indian Indentureship," as January 2020 marked the formal end of Indian
Indentureship globally.

** Usually, most people didn't know.

Not everything's written in the book.
So sometimes you gotta look to the margins for notes.

THE PERFORMER gestures to themself.

Like—you got any Indo-Caribbean friends?

*They wait for a reaction and responses. If no one else
does they simply state, "Cool, do you want one?" If
anyone does, THE PERFORMER uses the following text:*

Everybody else—do you want one?

Okay! So—now! The first Indo-Caribbean-Hindu-Canadian
identity play—*that we know of* . . . are we ready to make history tonight?

All right. Let's get started!

*THE PERFORMER triggers a new sound cue from the
laptop.**

Let's play a game. Shall we?
It's a call and response game.
Everybody down with that?

---

* We used "High Tide or Low Tide" by Bob Marley and the Wailers. This
could change, though there's something about it being a Bob Marley track
that speaks to a larger Caribbean diaspora while performing an aspect of
Hindu ritual that's kinda nice. It should be something mellow, nostalgic,
and decidedly Caribbean. And again, consistent.

THE PERFORMER should actively play this game with the audience, being responsive to what's happening in the room.

The dog says? . . .

The audience responds.

The cat says? . . .

The audience responds.

The goat says? . . .

The audience responds—likely with a fair amount of variation.

The cow says? . . .

The audience responds—most likely with "moo."

Ya. Okay. So you're wrong! I will fight you on that!

Now, to be fair, I'll chalk it up to a cultural translation thing. Because most of the cows that I know happen to be Trinidadian cows.
Much like myself. But we're gonna get into that in a little bit.

But see, I've always kinda thought that cows—at least Trini cows—they make a sound that's a lot more like:

"Neeeeeeeeeee!"*

And if you ignore them, or you annoy them or something?
They make this awesome sound where they go:

"NeeeeeeeeeaAAAAAAH!"**

And because I've always thought that the Trinidadian
accent kinda sounds like people are constantly whining and
complaining—
no offence to any Trinis here—but it kinda does!
I've always felt they're kinda going:

"Eh, boooooooooy,
Take d milk, naaaaaaaah? . . .
Taaaaake d milk, naaaaaaaaaah?
All yuh*** come and take d milk, nah? . . .
All yuh! . . .
All yuh! . . .
. . .
All yuh! . . .
All yuh come and take d milk, naaaaaaaaaah????!

---

*   My capacity in print fails to fully articulate what a cow sounds like.
But go listen to cows. They make very cool sounds. Rarely "moo."

**   This one is a belaboured cow sound. As if to say, "Come on!!!"—the
latter part goes a bit higher pitch.

***   All yuh is Trini vanacular for "all of you" or "you guys"—but it can
also be singular.

... OOOOOOOOOOOH GAAAAAAAAAAAWD!
How all'yuh ga treat me so!!?
All'yuh go and make me make de blasted milk and now
all'yuh go an' hold up yourself!!??

All yuh come and take de blasted milk, naaaaaaaaah!?????"
...

*(schups)** " ... 'Oman. Come and take de milk."***

Cows are fucking awesome.
I've known this since as far back as I can remember—
but I don't think I've always known why.

I do know that sometimes when I talk about cows
and someone makes a *cutesy* joke like:
"Mmmm ... cows. Yum"
—I have a visceral desire to break their face.

Which is weird.
'Cause I'm not really a violent person.

---

* This is a sound often called "kissing the teeth." It's a Caribbean thing—
kind of a sound implying "seriously? ... "

** "Oman" means "woman" in a Caribbean accent.

I'm like a . . . Caribbean dude. You know?
Laid back!
. . . Irie!
. . . Ganja!
Ba da ding ding dang dong doooooooooooo!*

So, ya . . . I'm none of that.
But I *am* Trinidadian.

And the first reaction I tend to get from people when I tell
them I'm Trinidadian is:
"But . . . you're not Black."

Except for in the Maritimes—where they still think I'm
Black.

And it's just amazing to me that you wouldn't just naturally
assume that there's a massive population of South Asians in
Trinidad—'cause there's pretty much a massive population of
South Asians . . . fucking everywhere!
We get around, man.
Pretty much anywhere the British went,
you know we were down to follow . . .

. . . And if by follow . . . You mean:

---

* This should be a failed attempt to do a reggae/dance hall vocal riff. It's
also referencing a Lonely Island sketch called "Ras Trent," which is just
. . . gold. They describe it as "a reggae song about the plight of being a
white, upperclass, Ivy League Rasta."

be subjected to imperial starvation policy in your homeland, and then, when faced with no other option but to attempt to survive, get ported off under false promises into indentured servitude to who the fuck knows where . . .

Or you know . . . *follow* . . .

Quote—Winston Churchill:

"I hate Indians. They are a beastly people with a beastly religion. The famine was their own fault for breeding like rabbits."

So, ya. I'm Trinidadian.
Specifically, I'm "Indo-" Trinidadian.
And apparently we got there 'cause we fuck like champs.

Other quote from Winston Churchill:

"I'm Winston Churchill. I'm a fucking cockface!"

Now, one of those quotes is historically accurate. But which one . . . I'll never tell.*

"Indians"—a beastly people . . .

---

* (Shhhhh . . . It was the first one. At least we haven't found direct recorded historical evidence that Churchill ever admitted to his cockfacery. I still hope one day we do, and if on that day there's still Churchill statues everywhere, we can replace the inscription to an amicable "Winston Cockface Churchill. British political leader during WWII, and general asshat to the subjects of the Empire. Fuck that guy.")

Now, in case anyone here is unfamiliar with what I mean when I say "indentured servitude," that's totally cool—I'll give you a primer.

THE PERFORMER triggers an upbeat backing track.[*]

So, basically—there's this thing called slavery.
And the British Empire was all about it.
Do I need to keep going? I'm gonna keep going—

So the British and other "colonial powers,"
which is a Western term for "assholes,"
started by enslaving local populations.
And then bought, kidnapped, and stole people and sent them
to the Caribbean to grow things like:
coffee . . . cocoa . . . and sugar.
Which I know sounds bad,
but you need to understand—they really liked sugar!

But, eventually, they decided that it was morally wrong to do so. Good job, Colonial Assholes!

I mean—it may have also had something to do with the people of Haiti, who between 1791 and 1804 *kicked the living shit* out of the "colonial powers"—putting an end to slavery in Haiti and declaring themselves their own soverign nation!

But you know . . . that's not *mainstream* history . . . That's just what happened.

---

[*] We used a South African (specifically Afrikaans) pennywhistle tune. It should sound like a bit of a sales jingle. Or, ya know, do what you want.

So—three years later—1807—British Empire—cockface king-
dom—starts the process of ending slavery for themselves.
Get a little bit sidetracked—they don't actually end it till 1833.
Except for in the British East India Company—where it continues for another ten years. Mainly in Sri Lanka.

But generally, in 1833, everybody agrees slavery is bad.
But *also* in 1833 the term *"servitude"* gets introduced.

See now, they've got all these islands in the Caribbean that
are full of people, who are now free, and understandably a bit
resentful of the people who used to *own them.*

So—they go to India.
Good timing 'cause there's a massive famine going on—which
if you recall is because we fuck like champs, and Winston
Churchill* is a cockface. His words.

So, say you are an Indian woman, in Bihar—where my family
comes from. Poor farming folk.
Somebody offers you a work contract!
You're gonna go to Calcutta—the capital at the time—serve a
wealthy family for a bit.
Pretty good deal, right?
All you gotta do is just sign this contract—which you
can't read—
and then boom! You are on a boat to Fiji, Mauritius, Guyana,
or Trinidad.**

---

* A.K.A. Winston "Cockface" Churchill.

** There's other places that the Indentureship extended to. These are
the ones I would mention due to larger populations and also because of
rhythm. But Indian Indentureship was huge. For example, almost every

But it's not slavery.
You do get paid.
You just have to work off the cost of travel.
And also the cost of living—which, by the way, you can only purchase food from the plantation you now work on.
And if you do anything that could be viewed as illegal—you can be immediately sent to jail without trial.
And I know that sounds bad—
but you have to remember—they really liked sugar.

THE PERFORMER brings the sound cue out.

But I want to be clear—it was not slavery.
I don't know if it was better, and I don't know if it was worse—honestly, to me it sounds better.
But I don't like to compare it.
Because that's what the British wanted us to do.
Indians and Africans.
They wanted to make sure we wouldn't get along.
And we are still paying for that today in the country that became home to us.

'Cause I've always felt that you don't get to say that you're truly from somewhere until your blood has mixed with soil.
And Indians? Africans? Asians? And of course the Indigenous Carib and Arawak people . . . our blood has drenched that island.

British colony in the Caribbean would be a destination. The reason I mention it is that for an audience hearing their specific heritage named has been quite impactful. So . . . if you know the community you're performing for, you might wanna shout some countries out.

But I will say this towards the Indentureship.
At least with the Indentureship
sometimes you got to keep your family.
Sometimes.

My last ancestor to leave India,
or what's now India,
was my great-grandfather.
And his name was Omkar Maraj.

Let me tell you a little about him.

    THE PERFORMER triggers a classic Hindi cinema tune.*

So, Omkar!
In this case he may not actually have been starved out.
I mean, maybe.
We don't actually know that much about him.
What we do know is that he was a *royal musician* . . . or a
musician, but he said he was royal, so we'll go with that.
He used to play music in one of the various princedoms
. . . somewhere in India . . .
. . . but uh . . . while I hate to ever support anything Winston
Churchill's ever said . . .
The fact was, Omkar . . . he had a way with . . . *the ladies.*

Apparently there was this village song they used to sing
about him back home that went something like:
"When Omkar comes around my waistband gets loose."

---

* This should have an element of nostalgia and warmth to it.

Which, if you were to translate that to today?
I think it means people were down to take him to red
lobster.*

And if you were to translate that to like 2005?
They'd take him to the candy shop!**

And if you translate that to like 1994?
He'd like it when you call him Big Poppa!***

Anyway, back in India . . . Omkar, let's say, "earned himself
a red lobster" . . . with a royal . . . And he got a price put on
his head.

But he was a noble guy.
He was an honourable man.
And he believed in fighting for the things he believed in.
And in this case?
That was: not being dead.

So he got his ass on a boat and he went all the way to
Trinidad. And I'm sure he had no idea where the fuck
that was.

And after he did his obligatory stint in the Indentureship . . .
He was actually able to buy himself out.

---

* That's a Beyoncé reference. Could be changed! But should capture the
feeling of "if my man fucks me good, I take him to Red Lobster."

** That's a 50 Cent reference.

*** That's a Biggie reference.

And what did he do?
Well, he had a cow.
He had a shop.
And he played music late into the night.

And I know, all that—it might not sound like a guy worth celebrating.
But it was people like that who were keeping the songs up from the villages back home?
It was people like that who kept our culture alive.

> *THE PERFORMER triggers a sound cue that fades into a filtered version of the existing sound that gradually dissappears, evoking the fading of memory.*
>
> *They unwrap the book and hold it in their hand.*

This is the *Ramcharitmanas*,[*]
an adaptation of the *Ramayana*, a great epic that was translated by the sage Tulsidas into the more common tongue.
And if you simplify and translate the message, it basically says:
"If you work hard,
And you do the right thing,
we will overcome the darkness of corruption and tyranny,
and light will return."

---

[*] I think there's something about actually having a copy of the *Ramcharitmanas* present as opposed to just any book. Again, do what you want, but books carry a lot of importance in my tradition.

And traditionally, it's sung.
This whole thing is a song.*
'Cause not everyone can read.
But people like music.

This is the kind of song he would have brought with him.

They carefully wrap the book back in its cloth.

From late nights by the fire in the dying crops of Bihar,
to late nights by the fire in the sugar cane fields of Trinidad.
Tradition.

See, I'm a Hindu.
Before being a *beastly* Indian, I'm a *beastly* Hindu.

And I don't think I ever really knew I was a Hindu in particular, until I was growing up in Dartmouth, Nova Scotia.
Wasn't really a big Hindu community there ...
The only other Hindus I knew I was related to—so the topic
of "Hindu identity" never really came up that much.

Except around Christmas time.
I used to routinely get into trouble for not wanting to sing
in the Christmas concert.
Something about it felt wrong to me.
And it's not because I have anything against Christianity.
It's just that, while they all got a concert—and basically the
entire month of December ...

---

* It's a really big book.

The only thing I ever learned about my religion in school was, one day, when I found a couple of pages in a book in the school library entitled: *The Encyclopaedia of Eastern Mythology.*

Referencing the altar.

Because apparently all the things I believed in were just myths.

A lot of Indians in Trinidad are Hindu.
There's also a lot of Muslims.
And a *ton* of Christians, because when the British were in charge, you technically *had* to be Christian if you wanted to do things like go to school or get married.

So that meant that Hindus and Muslims, we had to convert.
Or pretend to be Christian.
In the case of school, you had to pretend enough to convince the headmaster.

Now, Hindus, we're pretty cool with shouting out other people's gods,
we got plenty.
So they'd pretend to be Christian—and then they'd do their own thing at home.
If they were allowed to go home.

And if that sounds chillingly familiar to something
Canadian . . . * it's probably 'cause the missionary schools in
Trinidad that were specifically focused on Indians were run
by Canadians.
From Nova Scotia as it turns out.
And again, I'm not trying to compare—and please don't.
It's all shitty.
All I mean to say is Empire runs deep.

But you learned to play along if you could.
My dad. To this day he knows the "Lord's Prayer" by heart.
But he also knows the "Hanuman Chalisa."
And my auntie can sing *Ramayana*.
And my grandfather raised cows.
And they fucking loved those cows like family.

And that's the one thing people tend to know about Hindus.
We fucking *love* cows.
As a Hindu—you don't ever harm a cow.
'Cause that would be a Hin-don't.

---

* Here I'm referencing the Canadian Residential School System. The last
of which closed in 1996. To be clear, the missionary schools in Trinidad
run by John Morton from New Glasgow, Nova Scotia, do not have the
same known history of abuse as the Canadian system. Schools in other
colonies however, like Guyana, have been recorded to have done some
very messed up things. In fairness, my mother grew up in one of these
shools and overall had a good experience, though the objective remained
to convert "Hindoos" with hopes that if they went back to India they
would convert other Hindus there. Also, fuck John A. Macdonald. Tear
down all of his statues. If we need to commemorate something in Canada,
let's put up a statue of the cocktail napkin agreement of Confederation.
Seems as legit as the treaties, or lack thereof.

There's a lot of reasons for this. So, here's one from our stories . . . It's kinda like our version of the Big Bang. . . . Kinda.*

This is the story of the ocean of milk.

> *The lights shift as shadows of THE PERFORMER are cast on the curtains. They trigger the sound, underscored by a raga and hip hop inspired beat.***

All right, so there's this giant ocean of milk.
And at this time the demigods—or the "Devas"—and the demons—or the "Asuras"—are both in search of eternal life.
And at the bottom of this ocean is Amrita, the elixir of eternal life. In order to get it, you gotta churn the ocean.
Neither side is strong enough to churn it on their own.
So they decide they're gonna work together.

Now, what's the easiest way to churn an ocean of milk?
Well, you take a mountain and then flip it upside down.
Obviously.
See the goal is that they'll make this mountain spin.
And as it spins the ocean will start to churn.

---

* It's really not exactly the Big Bang at all. But a lot of the things we say in the show are as a point of translation to an equivalent that the audience might have some familiarity with. The Big Bang was the closest thing we could get to—and it's not *wrong*, per se—it's just perhaps more than that since it comes from a poem.

** We used an instrumental cut of MC Yogi and Krishna Das's "Jai Sita Ram"—again, could be anything—but what that track had that we really liked was the relative sparcity of a hip hop beat (for speaking over) with the inclusion of traditional instrumentation—like harmonium and tabla—that you would hear in puja.

But then the mountain starts to sink.
'Cause it's a mountain.

Then Vishnu—who's the god of preservation, by the way—
he's like: "Yo, I got this shit"—takes the form of a turtle.
Then on the back of the turtle, they put the mountain.

Still not working. It's gotta spin.

So then this massive Naga, this massive snakelike being
named Vasuki—Vasuki wraps himself around the mountain.
And on one side the Devas pulled, and on the other side the
Asuras pulled—and then as they pulled, back and forth—
back and forth—the ocean starts to churn.

And from this churning we get Amrita.* The elixir of eternal life.

Now here's the thing.
Both sides start to fight over this.
Thinking that one side deserved it more than the other.

---

* A note on Sanskrit—sometimes there's an "a" at the end of the word
"Amrita." When it's pronounced closer to "Am-reet" the "a" in "Amrita" is
still there, but barely pronounced. It's more like a hard "t." This is technically true of the word "Jiv," which is technically "Jiva"—just a heads up
when we get there.

And Vishnu, he's watching this all go down, so he takes
the form of a beautiful woman—which totally distracts the
demons.
Then his good pal Garuda—who's the king of the birds, by
the way—Garuda swoops in and takes the Amrita and gives
it to the gods. And that's why gods live forever.*

*THE PERFORMER triggers the sound out, and the lights
restore.*

Also the snake got some too.

And that's why snakes shed their skin and stay young
forever.
And are fucking terrifying.**

Pretty simplified version of the story, but you get the idea.

More practically though—Hindus love cows because cows
are fucking awesome.
Especially if you're poor.

---

* It's debatable if "gods live forever" in this sense. There's also a lot of
versions of the story. So, for example, in one sense, the demigods often
have planetary equivelents (i.e., the god/demigod Shani is Saturn). Some
sects see them as more or less eternal, other sects see them as definitely
not. Either way they live much longer than humans and most life on
earth. But, like . . . what is even life, bruv? . . .

** Snakes are terrifying. Don't try to convince me they're not. If you
have a pet snake you love, I respect that. But I will never come to your
house. (Not to assume an invitation was on offer.)

And by and large, historically in Trinidad:
Indians, Africans, Asians, Indigenous folk . . .
We all tended to be poor.
Probably because of that whole slavery . . . indentured
worker . . . genocide thing . . .

And while everyone tried to find a way out this poverty, the
way that is a big part of my heritage was very much the
strategy of Hindu South Asians—cows.
So yeah, I fucking love cows.

They give you milk,
They help you pull stuff,
And you can use their shit to build your house.
Literally.

All my family grew up in houses made of cow and/or bull-shit!
And one of the oldest temples in Trinidad,
that my great-grandfather cared for—
where people who were running away from the plantations—
from being raped and beaten in the plantations—they'd
go there for shelter—just to hide out for a while— It's still
there!

So you could say—that shit holds up!

So cows are great. They are the life of our people.
And all they ask for is some grass, and a pet on the head.

When my grandfather finally had enough money,
he bought a plot of land and they built a little cowshit hut
there where all eleven of them lived, and they raised cows.
Later, that would become the street where all my dad's
family lived, and the location of one of the first Hindu
schools, where kids could finally go to school without having
to change their religion.

But all the while, through all the years, there remained cows
on that back road.
Recently renamed "Pandit Parasram Road"—for my
grandfather.

Which sounds way more legit than what it used to be called:
"Behind the Hindu School, McBean Village."

My brothers were born there; they grew up there a bit.
My family's all from there.
But I—was born—here.

And growing up as the only member of an immigrant
family, who is technically not an immigrant can get a little
bit weird!

They used to call me the "white boy"?
'Cause I guess I talked a little different.
Which, since everyone else thought I was Black, was like—
extra confusing.

And then of course you get the assholes who'd be like:

"Hey, man! I don't even see you as a Black guy. I see you like a normal white guy!"

And I'd be like: "I am neither Black nor white!"

Besides! Like who wants to be white? Not even white people wanna be white anymore. Am I right, white people?
It's okay, we're all allies here!*

Anyway, I insisted that I was *Trinidadian*.

But that also meant I kinda had to prove it.
You know? That I was like—proper *"Third World"*?
With like—proper *"Third World skills"*?

    THE PERFORMER triggers a reggae horn.

Other kids had Game Boys!
I had a wheel that I proudly pushed with a stick!

    Reggae horn.

Other kids had yo-yos!
I had a bottlecap on a string that I hammered into a super sharp razor blade thing I used to cut people with!

    Reggae horn.

---

*   Usually people cheer or groan at the "am I right, white people" part. Rarely it's dead silent. In any case, whatever the reaction, "we're all allies" should be used in a way that acknowledges and teases the audience. Unless there's no white people. In which case . . . maybe try, "Don't tell them we know!"

And when I went down to Trinidad, I didn't get that typical Caribbean vacation getaway package.

You know this whole thing?

> *They trigger an excerpt of a Road March Carnival song.**

None of that shit for me, man! Nah!

For me—it would go a bit more like this:
The plane would land,
You'd get off the plane,
And then you are immediately slapped in the face with a wall of humidity—'cause this was before they had the connection to the airport, so you'd just walk right onto the tarmac.

And then I'd go see my uncles.
And they'd take me to see the cows.
Give me some fresh milk with sugar in it.
And let me tell you, there is nothing better than some fresh cow's milk with sugar in it.
I still have it sometimes . . .
You know, when I want to treat a Jiv.

Because my name is Jiv.

---

* A Road March is like a big Carnival hit. Carnival in the Caribbean sense of the biggest party ever. Ask your Caribbean friends what "Jump Up and Wave" means, they'll fill you in. We used an excerpt of the very popular soca/chutney mashup track "Come Beta" by Destra Garcia, featuring Shurwayne Winchester.

And then, as I was basking in my Third World glory—having done the arduous tasks of walking off a plane and drinking a cold beverage—my uncles would say:

"Fat boy."

'Cause Caribbean people are rude.

"Right, Fats. All yuh know how to lay pitch?"

And I'd be like: "Yeah. I know how to lay pitch."

I did not know what that meant.

But in fairness—*to me*—does anyone here know what laying pitch means?

> THE PERFORMER *surveys the room and has a legit conversation with anyone who wants to guess.*

So, pitch. Pitch is like naturally occurring asphalt. And "laying pitch" means fixing the road.

So here's how you lay pitch:

Step one—you take a twelve-year-old child—from Canada ... send him out in thirty-five-degree humid Trinidad.

Step two—you give him a shovel and a barrel full of pitch. No mask! No respiratory support!

Step three—body-shame him.

Step four—let him fix the road.

And that, my friends, is how you lay pitch.

Reggae horn.

And now all that may just sound like "child abuse"—

But you see, in the Third World, there's no such thing as child abuse.
'Cause child abuse is a First World problem.

Reggae horn.

So that's how it would go.
Fix the road? Fix the road!
Build a speed bump?
I didn't know you "built" speed bumps?
I didn't know why we needed one 'cause there were only five houses on the whole road . . . but sure! I'll build a speed bump!
Learn how to rewire the electrical in this house!
I did that. I now know how to do that.

Because I was *Proper Third World Legit.*

Or should I say . . . Proper Third World *LeJiv!*

> *If the audience isn't having it (which they likely are not 'cause it's a step too far in lacklustre puns) . . . sad reggae horn.*

This one time, my brother, he went down solo.
And he got, like, the holy grail of tasks.
See, one of the cows was *pregnant*.
And he helped it *deliver a calf*.
And then they *named the calf after him*!

And maybe it's just me,
but that is like being fucking canonized for a Hindu!

And you know—we were all proud of him.
But I was also kind of like:
"Fuck off, man! You're not even religious!"
Or not that—but kind of? I don't know . . . it wasn't fair, ya
know? He got to grow up there.
He got to hang out with my grandfather in the puja room.
I learned about who I am through *a coffee table book in a
school library*! I've had to fight for it.

But then! I'm about to head down—and my cousin calls me
and says, "One of the cows is pregnant . . . And it's due any
day now."

And I was like, FUCK YES!!!!!!

So as soon as I land, I don't say hi to anyone!
I just go straight to the cow.

> *THE PERFORMER triggers the Caribbean mellow tune, a
> reprise of the song at the beginning of the ritual.*

And there she is … Looking all big and pregnant and shit.
And I was like:
"Hey, cow.
Hey, cow friend.
Don't you worry about a thing.
I'm here.
We're in this together.
You and me.
Family connection."

And she was like:
"Neeeeeeeeahhhhh."

And I was like:
"Jiiiiiiiiiiv."
And then I fed her a big green bean.
'Cause cows love big green beans.

 THE PERFORMER brings the music out.

… They do.

So time went on, and on …
And I did all the regular stuff, you know?
Fix the road? Fix the road!
Paint the wall? Paint the wall!
Dig holes?—I don't know why we always had to dig holes—
but I dug the holes!

Then one night, it must have been like two? Three a.m.?
My cousin comes and wakes me up.

And I think ... this is it—the moment has come!

So we rush over. And this *was* it! You know?!
This is the moment I've been waiting for!
This was gonna be the full realization of my heritage!

And then the cow doctor—who is a doctor for cows—
the cow doctor says to me:
"Young boy, go and get some rope."

Which at first I think is kinda weird, but I've never delivered a calf before, so ... whatever. I go and get some rope.

I come back, rope in hand, and I give it to the cow doctor.
And I start to get a bit concerned because he's tying it into
this weird kind of lasso thing ... and I look over at the
cow, and she's in a lot of pain. Which I guess makes sense,
because she's giving birth—and I mean, has anyone here ever
given birth before?

> *THE PERFORMER should only lightly engage with the
> audience if they respond.*

Well, I hear it sucks. Or it's *beautiful*!

But very painful.

And I imagine it sucks even more when something's got a
giant head *and* horns coming out of you!

So, eventually, the cow doctor explains what's going on.

The calf wasn't coming.
The calf was inside but turned the wrong way.
And he was going to suffocate if we didn't get him out.
There wasn't enough time to do a C-section—
so this was gonna be our only chance.

Now shit got real.

What we had to do was go inside, turn the calf around, then
tie him with the rope, and pull him out.

Now, I don't know how many of you here have ever had your
hands inside a cow's vagina before?*

But while it's larger than say . . . a human vagina, it's still
not easy to get "all up in there" when there's a baby cow
trying to come out.

So, after the cow doctor tried, and my uncle tried, and my
cousin tried . . . it didn't look good . . .

But see, I've got this thing with my hands, right?
I'm a big guy—but I've got super flexible hands.
My thumbs? They bend *all* the way down.

   *THE PERFORMER demonstrates.***

---

* It's worth noting that so far there have been a *lot* of people who have
had their hands inside of a cow's vagina and let me know about it. Or at
least they really like to sit up front.

** They do in fact bend all the way down. Lots of people think it's gross.
I think it's cool. But I sure like grossing people out.

Ladies? . . . Gentlemen? . . .

So boom!
Here I am, right? Elbow deep in a cow's vagina!
I'm fulfilling my heritage!
Cows are holy, so I'm doing God's work.
The cow doctor's guiding me through it.

Aside.

And you have to understand, there's a lot on the line here!
I am reaching into the darkness of this cow's vagina,
searching for what?
A calf?
No! More than that!
My identity!
No more "white boy,"
No more "Canadian"—
I could be a true Indo-Trinidadian—I could *be* proper
Third World. I could be like my brother—be part of this
family—and then—

Back into it.

I can feel the calf's head.

So I start trying to turn this thing around. But it's like it
doesn't want to turn. But I keep turning and turning, but
it's like it doesn't want to be born.
But I try, and I try . . . and finally it starts to turn!
And I think: YES! I got it! I got you, cow!

We tie it with the rope.
Then all of us, we're in this intense tug of war, pulling and
pulling for everything we're worth.

Aside.

And it's kind of absurd.
Like, if you were to see it—it would have looked like four
grown-ass men pulling a rope out of a cow's vagina.
And that's because it was four grown-ass men pulling a rope
out of a cow's vagina!

Back into it:

So we're pulling and we're pulling,
And the mama cow's crying,
and we're pulling,
and she's crying,
and the baby won't come!
And we're pulling—just trying to bring life—bring this poor
calf, this member of our family out into the world!
And I just start getting livid!
Like: "Little brother! You! Yes you, cow! You listen to me!
You are the lifeblood of our people! Do you understand me?!
You are life!
So GIVE ME LIFE!"

And in my head, I just have this flash:

THE PERFORMER triggers some spacey, ambient music.

Amrita—the elixir of eternal life—the ocean of milk . . .
And Vishnu took the form of a turtle,
and on the turtle's back, a mountain was placed.
And around that mountain was coiled a massive Naga, a
massive snake . . .
And on one side the Asuras pulled and on one side the
Devas pulled . . .
Good and Evil . . . light and dark . . . together.
And from their pulling, the ocean churned and never-ending
life was born . . . Between life and death . . . is eternal life . . .

And then . . . as I'm having this deep . . . religious
. . . philosophic . . . epiphany . . . I remember—

THE PERFORMER snaps out the music.

Fuck! There's a cow!

So we're pulling, and we're pulling,
and the mama cow's crying!
And we're pulling, and she's crying, and we're pulling—
and then it gets to the point where we have to make a
choice! Because she's so tired.
The mother cow is so tired . . .
And if we keep going she's not gonna make it.
But I could see the legs!

. . .

The calf died. Didn't make it . . .
And I never got to fulfill my heritage . . .
But it's not about that.

See, I was chasing this dream? About all the things I'm sup-
posed to be . . . all that shit.
And chasing dreams can be a very selfish thing to do.
Maybe not "selfish"—but like "self-ish."
It's easy to forget that it's not about you. 'Cause it's not
about me.

You know, in the story, that's how we lost eternal life.
For me . . . well, I lost a calf. I lost a brother . . .
It's easy to lose sight of what's important.

The next day, I went by my uncle's, and the mother cow, was
there . . . She didn't make that "Trini cow" sound.
I asked my uncle about it. And he said: "She's grieving."

So, I didn't get a calf named after me.
But I spent the summer with that mother cow.
And I sat with her in her grief.
I may have had to lose my brother,
but at least I could keep my auntie.

> THE PERFORMER *returns to the altar. He sprinkles*
> *water, takes water in his hands, and then drinks. He*
> *performs aarti* for the bottle of milk with the incense.*
> *He pours the milk, but as it touches the glass, the milk*
> *turns black. He stares into it as the lights focus in.*
> *Then suddenly:*
>
> *Black—* THE PERFORMER *and the entire stage disap-*
> *pear. An intense layered sound score plays as lights*

---

* Ritually circling three times clockwise.

> *blind the audience. The sounds of a gong? A low*
> *rumble? A screaming star? In the nothingness we hear:*

And it would be nice if it ended there. Right?
Nice Hindu boy goes back to Trinidad and finds his
identity . . .

I mean that's nice. Digestible . . .
All you had to do was sit there and passively take in my
culture.

But we did all agree to make history . . .

To make an Indo-Caribbean-Hindu-Canadian identity play.

Soooooooooo . . . We're not done yet . . .

Reincarnation, man, we just keep coming back.

Here's the thing:
a Hindu can't do an identity play.
'Cause identity is a Hin-don't.

Identity means that there is an identifiable divide between
things—where one thing ends and another begins.

And see, Hinduism teaches that these divisions are . . . an
illusion. What we call Maya.
That this whole existence itself is just a dream of the great
cosmic consciousness.

Identity is an illusion.

And so this play, this whole play, this whole genre of plays,
in a manner of speaking has been about . . . nothing.

Because, for Hindus, true identity is . . . a field.
It's just a field.
And we strive to look at the field
and see a blade of grass and think:
"I am that blade of grass."
And what's in the field?
A cow.
And the cow is the blade of grass.
And you are the cow.

Because we are all the field.
And identity just divides that field.
Property.
That colonial concept: property.
Identity is just property.
Yours and mine.
And identity plays are just there to map it.
Secure the borders.

Did you come here to see an identity play?
Did you come here to watch me recolonize my thinking?
To partition it off to you in a digestible way so you too can
feel assured at what the borders are between me and you?

I mean . . . in fairness, that's how it was marketed . . .*
So like . . . our bad too . . .

---

* And it certainly was the first time we did it!

'Cause I can't do that . . .
I won't do that . . .
I won't draw those borders . . .

Identity is a Hin-don't because identity is an illusion.
That is a core belief I hold as a Hindu.
But in order to maintain that belief I need to hold onto my
identity.

But part of my belief says that identity is an illusion.

So by that definition I also believe that I shouldn't hold onto
my identity.

But if I don't hold onto my identity then I would just get
sucked into the mainstream belief system, which doesn't recognize that identity is in fact just an illusion!

So I need to identify myself, to identify identity as being an
illusion!

But identity is . . . an illusion! And that is a Hin-don't!
But I wanna be a Hin-DO!

'Cause all I know is that we strive to look at a field and just
chill!

So for the rest of this show—you can enter my mind!
That's what we're gonna do!
You can enter my mind and chill the fuck out!

Lights up. The stage has transformed—the curtains are gone, the stage is open with only the altar remaining. The floor is ablaze—lighting a shiva-incarnate Yantra, revealing the full pattern on the floor that was obscured before. JIV stands centre stage in a pool of light—chewing cud like cow. He is wearing a cow-print sherwani, lookin' like a bovine boss.

The sound blares some psychedelic rock. *

Mooooooooooo**
Is this what you wanted?
Mooooooooooooo!
Is this what you had in mind?
Ent all'yuh did come to take d milk?
Now all'yuh ga take d milk, nah?
Moooooooooooooaaaaaaaaaaaah!

> *The stage dips to black as JIV appears at the lip of the stage.*

Do you feel cultured?
Have you consumed enough of my culture?
Do you like my diaspora?
Do you want to touch it?
Too bad! You can't! It's intangible!
Fucking George Harrison and shit!
Ravi Shankar!
Sai Baba!

---

* We used Cream's "White Room."

** I know I wrote "mooo" here. It's the same cow sounds as before.

Hare Krishna!
Amitabh Bachchan Zindabad!*

The stage dips to black as JIV appears behind the altar.

You wanna report back to your yoga class that you came and felt enlightened?
Take the fucking milk, naaaaaaaaaaah?

JAI SHIVA SHAKTI!
OM NAMAH SHIVAI!
EVERY STEP!
EVERY LINE IN THE SAND THAT YOU DRAW TO SAY THAT I AM NOT YOU WILL BE DESTROYED!
ALL WILL FALL TO ASH!
TAKE D FUCKIN' MILK NAAAAAAAH?!
OOOH GAAAAAAAAAAAAAAAAAWD!

The stage dips to black. JIV appears at the back corner of the stage. Apparently floating. There is a pulsing drone. He looks around. Opens his mouth and points to it.

Hey. You're in my mind now . . .
This is what it's like . . .
Welcome to my mind.

---

* I owe this line to Munish Sharma, who apparently once climbed a mountain as a kid while cheering this. Which is hilarious to me. (Amitabh Bachchan is a major Bollywood star, with temples and stuff dedicated to him.)

JIV steps off the box and crosses the stage—right, actually he wasn't floating, he was just standing on a box ... He opens his mouth again and points to it.

This is what a Hindu's mind is like ...
We all wanted to know ...

JIV crosses to the lip of the stage.

... Now here we are ...

He does that mouth thing again.

One sec ...

He clicks a button on the computer, bringing the pulsing drone out.

I just really like that track.

This next section is somewhat improvised with the audience each night, singling out individual audience members.

Hey—what's your name?

The audience member responds.

That's good.
Hey, what's better, cows or horses?

The audience member responds.

Cool. Cool cool cool cool cool . . .

Hey—what's your name?

The audience member responds.

That's good.
What's better, puppies or kittens?

The audience member responds.

Cool. Cool cool cool cool cool . . .

Hey—what's your name?

Et cetera.

That's good.
What's better, colonialism or imperialism?

If they don't know:

Okay. But the world's binary though. You gotta choose one.
0101001001.

Hey—what's your name?
That's good.
Do you know what Jiv means?

Jiv comes from Jivatman.
And the Atman is the great cosmic supreme consciousness.
And the Jivatman is the aspect of that supreme conscious-
ness that lives within all of us . . . Pretty cool, huh?

Ya . . . Jiv's pretty cool . . .

So, did you know that you are also Jiv?
Are you cool with that?
Cool! Cool cool cool cool!

Hey—what's your name?
Did you know that you are also Jiv?
You cool with that?
Cool! Cool cool cool cool cool!

Hey what's your name?
Or another name for ____ might be?

> *It's Jiv.*

Nice. We are all Jiv.

> *JIV continues this until people accept they are Jiv.*

Hey!

> *Now to everyone:*

You guys like Lauryn Hill?

*JIV triggers music: Lauryn Hill's "Everything is Everything."**

I like Lauryn Hill.
Interesting fact: Lauryn Hill—also a Jiv.

Hey—what's your name?

It's Jiv.

Would you rather be a donkey or a mule?**
Nice—and what do those two things have in common?

They're both Jiv.

Ya, we are all Jiv.

Hey! Would you rather be a kangaroo or a wallaby?
Doesn't really matter because what do those things have in common?

They are both Jiv.

That's right, they are both Jiv!
Also marsupials. Marsupials, also Jiv.

Hey! Would you rather be a raccoon or a Toronto raccoon?***

---

*   I suppose you could use *not* this song . . . but it's pretty perfect.

**   With all of these there should be some minor banter.

***   This one we change depending on where we're performing. For example, in Vancouver we did "A seagull or one of those big-ass Granville Island

The banter continues. A key aspect should be that it's high energy and affirming. Like if Bruce Dickinson* was giving you a motivational speech.

Hey! Would you rather be a dung beetle or a tapeworm?

He starts pointing around to many people.

Hey, who's that over there?

It's Jiv.

Nice!

Who's that up there?

It's Jiv.

Who's that in the back?

It's Jiv.

It's Jiv!

What do we call *this* side of the audience?
Jiv!

---

fry-stealing seagulls." In Ottawa we did "Brownface Trudeau or Blackface Trudeau." That one was my favourite.

*   Front man of Iron Maiden.

And what do we call *this* side of the audience?
Jiv!

What do we call those people up in the booth?
Jiv!

What are we?
Jiv!

What's our name?
Jiv!

What are all of us?
Jiv!

Then let's say it together now:
Everything is every—
Jiv!

> *JIV triggers the sound out.*

Ya—I like Lauryn Hill. She's a good Jiv ...

> *Without even a veiled attempt at a transition in thought:*

Maaaaaaaaaaan, I didn't want to do an identity play.
I didn't want to do an identity play because identity is just
a raft.
And I know I said it was a field earlier,
but I guess it doesn't matter—
'cause like everything is everything, right?
Every Jiv is every Jiv.

But I think raft is more to the point.

Because even though it's all an illusion—identities are real because this is not a world where we can ignore difference.

I said earlier—I don't think states are real.
Borders? Not real!
You know who thinks borders are real?
Border guards.
And they got guns!

So ya, even though it's all an illusion ... here we are
... living through the illusion.

JIV looks at a stool placed stage right.

I'm gonna go sit on that stool and talk to you all serious
... like LeVar Burton on *Reading Rainbow* ...

*He goes to the stool, presumably to talk to the audience
all serious like LeVar Burton on* Reading Rainbow.

When I was growing up in Nova Scotia,
I wanted Nova Scotian identity.
I wanted in on that raft.
I wanted to be part of that mainstream.

I wanted to be that—but how could I?
I was neither Black nor white.
Neither Black nor white in a place that was divided.
For good reason.

Now, white people loved to talk about how great they were—
and how the Underground Railroad ended in Nova Scotia.
Which it did! The mainstream history . . .
What they didn't like to talk about was Africville.
The marginal history . . .

If you're unfamiliar—
Africville was a free settlement of Black people that was
growing . . . growing too close to the otherwise white
downtown.

And up on that mainstream white raft, they do not talk
about Africville.
Especially how the white government bulldozed Africville
and scattered the people to the margins of society.

And sure, you can look at that and say:
"Look at what Nova Scotians did to themselves.
We hurt each other.
Jiv hurt Jiv.
Jiv on Jiv violence."

But that's not what really went down, was it?

It was always difficult to determine exactly which raft I
belonged on in the first place.
'Cause everybody else, Mi'kmaq, Asians, Arabs, Jews—all
the other others—we disappeared from that binary regional
consciousness.
We were at the margins of the margins,
in a dichotomous Black and white world.

And because of this, the less I identified with Black people,
the more I was allowed on the white side.
On the mainstream Nova Scotian raft.
But here's the trade-off:
the less I talked about the realities that affected Black
people,
the more I let that history be forgotten.

And let's face it, I was just hanging off the edge of that white
mainstream Nova Scotian raft anyway.
I was tolerable.
... 'Cause Indians ... we're good at keeping our head down.
Ahimsa.
Non-violence.
Gandhi ...
We keep to ourselves.
We take care of ourselves.
And adapt to the system around us to survive.
And at least this way I wasn't left alone to float downstream!

But identities shift—and the raft fractures ...

For me that happened in junior high school.
Early 2000s ... Early school year—the leaves hadn't
changed ...
Must have been ... September ... maybe the ninth or the
twelfth ...
Or maybe it was September 11, 2001.

My whole life I was different—but acceptable.
But then this kid told me that someone flew a plane into the
Twin Towers—and we all ran to the school library window—
to watch the teachers watch the news.
And then one of the teachers—a young guy—a cool guy—he
came to the window.
And I saw him see me, and I saw something in his eyes
change. Then he shut the blinds.

I thought there'd be a war. I thought—I'm gonna go to war!
Defend my country! Protect my home!
But that's not how it went . . .
Instead my teachers would ask me about my uncle Saddam
and Bin Laden in class . . . And I got frustrated—'cause the
raft was getting rocky.

JIV stands.

Instead my vice principal decided that I was a threat to
the student body and gave me the maximum suspension—
because I wasn't stable.

See, I had to make a word search in French class—'cause
that's what passes for education out east—and I put the
words "torche," or torch, with "voyageur"—together joined on
the O.
And my vice principal said I was threatening his Acadian
heritage, 'cause he was descended from the voyageurs and
clearly I wanted to torch them.

Just a reminder that I'm just some dangerous foreigner.
'Cause home is not where you live.
Home is where your blood has mixed with the soil.

JIV moves to downstage centre.

So it's late.
I've been isolated.
I'm depressed, so I sleep late into the day.
My mom and my brothers, they work at night.
My dad's working in Trinidad at this point—so I don't see
anyone for what feels like a real long time.
None of the other kids want to talk to me online anymore,
so I make a witty away message for my ICQ and I go for
a walk.

JIV moves up and around the altar.

As I'm walking up the street, this car drives by, and a guy
throws an egg at me and yells: "Nigger!"*

And I think: "Dude, man! Could you please be more accurate
with your racism? Call me Coolie! Call me Paki!"
But whatever . . . I keep walking.

---

* It was noted to me by an audience member (of the Indo-Caribbean
diaspora like myself) that me using this word was off-putting due to
the violence attached to it, and that I do not have a right to use it. This
is true, because even though this word has been used "against" me, it
does not carry the same weight because it is more often than not used
incorrectly by the persons hurling it at me. We decided to keep it in for
the purposes of storytelling and recounting this specific incident, but
to be clear—outside of its utility here, its familiarity is not something I
would prefer to propogate.

Cut up behind the old church to get to the park.
There's this guy smoking in the distance.
I don't think much of it.
But then I hear the word "Paki!" and I think:
"Heeeey! Progress!" And then I hear the word "terrorist."

And then boom.

    JIV runs his hand through the soil on the altar.

I'm on the ground.
My head smashed against a slatey Nova Scotian rock.
Time slows down . . . I watch my blood mix with the soil and
think: "I guess I'm home now . . . Guess this is what it means
to be home . . . "

I get back up.
He comes at me again.
I get his arm, I feel it go snap!
And I run.

I don't tell anybody about that for a long time.
I don't tell my family . . . They've got enough on their plate.
But when I do try to tell friends, teachers, other people—
they all say the same thing:
"Oh, there's no way that could have happened here."
Or: "Well, you do look pretty intimidating . . . "

'Cause identities shift. And the raft fractures.

See, I wasn't on the white raft anymore. I wasn't on the mainstream Nova Scotian raft.
Couldn't swim to the Black raft—and why should they take me in, anyway? What ounce of solidarity did I ever risk?

So I took the only raft I had left: Hindu.
And I don't know if I did that because of a truth I knew inside,
or just to draw a line and say: "I am not Muslim."
As if the people ignorant enough to hold that kind of hate would be able to tell the difference.

And I failed my Muslim brothers and sisters that day,
I failed my Muslim aunties and uncles . . .

Because I never said that this irrational hate was wrong.

In identifying as a Hindu, all I did was say—to the people who cast me off—"I am not the thing you hate. Please don't leave me here adrift. Take me back!"

When someone drew a line to say, "You are other!"?
My reaction was to draw another line and say, "But I'm not them!"

I failed because that reaction speaks to a larger legacy of colonization,
an Empire that had infected my mind to have me beg for the privilege to belong, even if it comes at the expense of others.

An Empire that will burn your humble moisture-farming family alive.

JIV returns to the lip of the stage.

You guys remember the Tiwana family in Alberta?
Sikh family who were burned alive in their family-run hotel?
Wasn't a lot of coverage in the news ...
There was a bunch of racist graffiti on the walls, but police refused to call it a hate crime ...
On the plus side they didn't all die.
On the downside, the sons got pretty sick from the smoke inhalation ... as they were pulling their father's burning corpse from the flames.[*]

I think one of the ways that Empire keeps itself alive is by ensuring that the people in the margins are too immobilized to rise up. To unify!

'Cause we wouldn't want another Haiti, would we?

Lights raise on the glass of black milk. JIV moves towards it.

The sound is now acting on its own—a slow, meditative march with the sound of cows.

---

[*] This is referencing the burning of a family's motel business in Bashaw, Alberta, in 2016. At the time of doing the shows there remained no real shortage of incidents of race-related violence against Brown people in Canada that could be swapped out. I do not have any communication with the family, and am drawing on the very limited news coverage.

When they churned the ocean of milk,
it wasn't just the elixir
of eternal life that came out.
There was also poison.
Halahala it was called.

    JIV references the liquid in the glass.

In the process of trying to achieve immortality,
the gods and demons churned out a poison that threatened
all existence.

It was the poison of their conflict.
Of their division from each other, the gods and the demons.
'Cause in Hinduism, you know what the difference is
between gods and demons when you get right down to it?

Nothing.

It's just light and dark . . . we only tend to think light is
better because we can see it. Seems truthful like that.

So when the poison came out—
They asked Shiva,
Mahadev,
the great supreme being,
god of destruction—
they prayed for destruction to save all existence.
And Shiva drank the poison.
And then Parvati,
his Shakti,
the earth,

his feminine form,
the only one more powerful than him,
she held his throat so he wouldn't swallow it and be
destroyed.

And together they held the venom,
all the hate and malice, born from the illusion of
difference . . .
so that the Amrita, the healing, could come.

You know . . . There's an old saying:
Before you can take the Amrita—before you can take
the milk?
You gotta take the poison . . .

> JIV *drinks the black liquid. Slowly he moves to the back*
> *wall and is pressed against it as the sound bleeds out.*

Do you know what it means to be marginal?

And if you don't know what I mean by that—that's okay.
Let me do my best to explain.

There is a labour to listening.

Reading between the lines.

A hyper awareness.

Because it's not violent—not outright.
Weirdly, that would actually be easier.
'Cause physical violence heals. Believe me. It heals.
Spiritual violence, however . . .

Will they let slip some microaggression to indicate—

To let you know—perhaps unknowing that they *are* letting
you know—that you are in fact beneath them?
That your experience . . .
perspective . . .
system of perception is . . . invalid?

They're not trying to inflame you . . . you know that.
But maybe they'd be content to extinguish you . . .

Here's one for me:
"Oh, I'm sure that's brilliant—but that is so esoteric I can't
possibly wrap my head around it."
Which translates maybe to:
"It's not worth my time to try to understand your way of
thinking." . . . My way of being.

And so you listen—and you mark that:
Check, noted.

"Well my other Brown friend said that's not her experience."
Check, noted.

Let's admit it, all religion is oppressive by nature.
Check, noted

No one else seems to have a problem, maybe it's just you?

. . .

And this listening . . . it takes energy.

But you have to listen, because you wouldn't want to falsely
accuse someone of something they're not doing.

                              Unless they are.

But they might not know they're doing it . . .

                              But it takes so much
                              energy to explain it
                              to them.

. . . But then how else will they know?

So it's now a judgment call—and it's all so draining—and you
can't fully engage—'cause you're on the fence—as to if this is
someone you can trust . . . and you can't be in the room—

And: "Hey—just checking in—it seems like you're not really
present? And the rest of us here—"

'Cause it's like you're wrapped up in your own thoughts—and
maybe it is all in your head? . . .

*Lights shift. JIV is in a tight container of light. There
are ambient streetcar sounds.*

And now I'm on the streetcar,
and the sound is too much
because I've been listening all day long.

And I put my hands over my eyes,
like this,
'cause I feel like I'm being watched.

No, not watched—I've been watching—I've been watching
and observing so carefully—reading between every line . . .

And my eyes are sore, and worn, and bursting out, and hot!
And my hands are cold 'cause the blood's drained from them
and I just want to cool my eyes down for a bit . . .

*Lights shift—as if in a hallway in a house party. There
are ambient party sounds lightly underscored by "chill
white hipster music."**

And now I'm in a new space . . . a friendly space!
A white friendly space! With friendly white people!
Good people, I'm sure . . . but I'm so tired, I can't know for
sure . . .
I can't keep up the listening, and the watching . . .

---

*   We used "New Slang" by the Shins as the "nicest, whitest, hipsterest
song ever"—Graham Isador wins for that call, if I remember it right.
Technically I guess now it would be Fleet Foxes . . . but I can't stand
them, even ironically.

My breath is getting shallow . . . I can't seem to breathe deep
enough to ground myself—and if I do it'll just look like some
kinda yogic breath control!
. . . They want to know about my scarf . . . they touch it
. . . they tell me they have one just like it . . .

> *Lights shift—back to the streetcar—a piercing, high-
> pitch drone slowly rises.*

The kid on the streetcar is staring at me—

Look, Mommy, a Coolie.*

And I'm so tired I'm shaking.

Look, Mommy, the Coolie is shaking,

She's not even saying Coolie—she doesn't know that word,
Maybe it's all in my head,
I can't seem to compartmentalize,
it's not my strength.
I'm exposed,
I feel cold,
I'm shaking . . .

Mommy, the man looks angry. Mommy, I'm scared!

And I am frightening!

---

* This next section is a direct adaptation from Frantz Fanon's *Black
Skin, White Masks*.

Sudden silence.

Because I do not belong . . .

Because to be marginal is to live with a nervous condition.

And to be fragile is to experience that condition anew—when you break down and watch your identity fragment like shrapnel come back to the vein . . .
'Cause you couldn't listen closely enough—for long enough—with enough endurance—to navigate the shitstorm of the mainstream. The main body of the text . . .

To be marginal is to live on the sides—

Always watching from the sides—making sure that *this* is worth your time—
Making sure that *they* won't purge you . . .

And you *are* immobilized in your margin, with the fear that there is nothing out *there* . . .

So, if that's all completely unfamiliar to you.
If you never have to feel marginal.
If you feel like you don't have to hold that poison on the daily . . .

I need you to go out there.
I need you to go outside . . .
For just five/ten minutes or so.

I just need a space where I can talk to the folks who also have to live on the sides.

I'll get the door for you.*

    JIV opens the door.

And if you have any mobility issues, please stay, you are most welcome to stay.

---

*   So, for the reader, if you identify with having the described "marginal" experience, you should keep on reading. If not, you can skip ahead to page 93.

And also, I want to be clear, identities are intersectional. I really don't know your lived experiences. So you're the only person who can say if you should stay or if you should go.* But if you experience that nervous condition, then by all means please feel welcome to stay—and if you don't then if you can help us create this space, that would be awesome.

Here, I'll play you some exit music.

> *JIV plays the "nostalgic" track again as the mainstream audience exists.*

---

* Or, in this case, keep reading.

So, if the reason you're staying is 'cause you're a super woke ally, I'll just remind you that allyship and allyhood is not static. It's not a badge you earn, it's an evolving practice. So right now there's an ask of allies that do not have this experience to help make the space, so you might need to leave.

If the reason you're staying is 'cause you're a super woke ally . . .

You might need to be super woke enough to get the fuck out of here.

Please identify as you will—this next section is meant for those who experience a lived experience in the margins. If you do not have that experience or choose not to identify as so, do not read the next section. You can pick it back up at page 93. Or, ya know, do what you want. Just know that if you choose to disrespect this ask, you consciously chose to disrespect that ask.

This section is often rewritten depending on the location and context. But this is the most consistent of what we tend to say here:

Wow . . . They're really gone . . .

Do you feel that? How the space has changed?
It's kind of like there's a loss? . . .
Maybe it's kinda sad? . . .
Maybe it's kinda like . . .

> *JIV triggers the sound of a reggae horn and plays a Road March song.*

RIGHT??! FUCKING RIGHT??!!
TAKE UP SOME SPAAAAAACE!
DON'T APOLOGIZE FOR THE SPACE YOU TAKE UP!!

Seriously, though, anybody feel weird about separating the audience like that?

I get it. I mean, like maybe you have friends out there.
Or your partner?
Or your brother?
Or you parent?
I don't know, right?

Like, I feel a bit weird about it too.
I mean, look—I have mainstream friends.
Some of my best friends are mainstream.

Anybody feel good about it?
Right. 'Cause I get that too, you know?
Bunch of marginal people, hanging out together . . .
Being marginal . . .

Okay, so here's the deal.
Here's the reason I asked the mainstream people—the
self-identified mainstream people—to step outside for a bit:
There are certain conversations that can be had in a room
with a bunch of people with a marginal experience that
cannot happen in the same way in a room with a bunch of
people with a mainstream experience.

'Cause they might think I'm talking on your behalf.
And when I say your behalf, I mean like all of us.

Also, it's still a play, so when I say "conversations"?
I mean, I'm still gonna just keep talking at ya for a while.
So here we go:

Here's my real problem with identity plays.
Every time I see one, it's all translation.
You get a marginalized body on stage, and then they spend
the whole time explaining their marginal identity to a
mainstream audience and then there's no time to get into
anything that's actually challenging or thought-provoking
for the people on the margins.

So we get to watch, and go—aw yeah . . . I relate to that.
Or . . . I feel represented?

And look—that is important. Representation is important. But wouldn't it be better if we could be represented and also talk about some real shit?

The way I see it, if I'm gonna take the time—*and* the tax dollars—*your* tax dollars, by the way—to make a show about marginal identity, I'd really rather it be a show that can actually offer something to the people who live in the margins rather than just another show where the mainstream "get to learn."

So here's my problem with marginal identity.
It implies that you have no power.
And that is wrong.
You have power.
We all have power.
And ya, some people here have more power than others, 'cause idenities are intersectional.
We're not all *equal* just 'cause we're all "marginal."
I am arguably the most powerful person in this room right now. I'm a cis straight dude on stage.
With a mic!
. . . With two mics. I have another one back there . . .

So, here's my problem with marginal *identity.*
When marginalization becomes *part* of your identity.
White supremacists—and stay with me on this—
white supremacists believe that they are being oppressed.

When I was growing up in Dartmouth, I was friends with a white supremacist. Which I know is kinda weird. I guess we were more acquaintances; also, he tazed me one time. It was at a party—Dartmouth is a weird place—anyway, for whatever reason he liked me.

His point was that he respected that there was Black power, so why shouldn't there be white power?

And sure, you could look at that and go: "Look around ya, fucking dumbass!"

Or you could look at that and say: "Well—this guy actually believes he's being oppressed."

Because what happens when we hang on to *that* mentality. That *marginalized* mentality—that we all just said we experience in some form . . .

. . . 'Cause, look, you know that marginal nervous condition? I hold that poison so often I don't know if I can turn it off. Even when I'm here with you . . . all my marginal people . . . I can't turn it off.

And I want to.

So what's the end goal?

Do we wanna be them?

Do we wanna be something else?

Because we *have* power.

But what happens when we've had our head down so long that we don't realize our power has grown?

People tend to think of Hindus as pretty passive . . .
Om Shanti Shanti?
Bhakti?
Yoga?
Bikram . . .
Hatha . . .
Ashtanga . . .
Hot?

For a long time in India, Hinduism was a marginal religion.
It was marginal *despite* being the majority.
But when the British left it became a Hindu state.
And then what happened?
They'd held that venom for so long it gave rise to Hindu
nationalism.

To this day, Hindus—believing that India is for Hindus—will
burn Muslim villages. Will murder. Will oppress—because
they *think* they're under threat.*

And look, I'm no Hindu nationalist, but let's face it: when
push came to shove—when I was a kid with my head
smashed open—I drew that line and I kicked whoever I
needed to off my raft.
And you know what?
I don't hold guilt for that.
'Cause I don't think guilt is productive.
That's a thing I did—and now that's a thing I need to work
hard every day to never do again.
'Cause that is the danger of the margins.

---

* And for the record—fuck Modi and the BJP too.

That we can be so distracted by staring into the main-stream—so enwrapped by the nervous condition—that we can't see beyond ourselves.
And then we become poisoned.

We keep to our side.
We take care of ourselves—*really* practise self-care—we have to! But maybe enough so that it gives us an out?
To say, "Well, I can't do anything about that, those main-stream fuckers fucked it up." And ya, they did—but it's not like we're not part of that too.

I don't think we can hold the venom individually, without succumbing to the poison . . . but maybe if we spread it out we can all be a little bit better?

Don't we wanna heal?
Sometimes healing doesn't feel good.

'Cause I know that we're not them.
But we're also them.
We might be on the margins of the page . . . but we're still on the page.

'Cause we are all Jiv, man.

. . . Anyway, that's what I wanted to say to you, but I felt like with all the mainstream folks here, there wouldn't be enough room on the page to get it all out.
So thank you for continuing to listen to me talk at you.
I'm gonna bring them back in if that's okay?

*JIV checks in with the audience, and when they're cool
with it:*

Okay. Cool.

Right! And just before I do . . . we're uh . . . we're gonna hand
out some party hats?
'Cause we might as well fuck with them a little bit, right?
Like how often do we get to do this?

*Party hats are handed out.**

Right! And guys—guys—one more thing!
. . . If you fucking tell anyone about this? . . .

*JIV triggers a track from the laptop** while making a
threatening "throat slice" gesture.*

Just kidding, do what you want, dudes.

---

* We thought about trying to include party hats in the publication,
but it seemed a bit wasteful, and also would make the cost of this book
higher, which we're pretty against. Do feel free to righteously craft your
own party hat out of whatever material you have. In fact, if you're reading
this in public, make one and put it on. Don't worry what anyone thinks.
Let them stare. Let them stare at your majesty!

** We used "Informer" by Snow.

The self-identified "mainstream" audience re-enters.
People who stayed behind are all wearing party hats.
Snow's "Informer" blasts from the speakers. Once every-
one is back:

There is always Snow in an identity play.

Here we are, everybody! Back together again . . . Some people
have party hats . . . some people don't . . . but it's okay! We're
all allies here!

I'm gonna take mine off.
You can do whatever you like with yours.
Because you have agency.

JIV puts his hat away and addresses the full audience.

Thanks for coming back, folks!
You know, when we were making this show and I told
people I thought there was gonna be a point where we had
to seperate the audience for a bit, a lot of people really didn't
think it was a good idea. And they *really* didn't think you'd
come back!
But you did.
And I think that says a lot.

So, let me give you some context on why we did that, and
why I think it's so awesome that you helped us make the
space to be able to do that.

So, for those of you who thought it was so you could go
outside and really understand what it feels like to be a marginalized person . . . It's not that—you were outside for like
five, seven minutes—it's not *quite* the same thing.

It's just that part of the show was not made for you.
And if that's troubling to you at all, then ask yourself how
often you encounter spaces that *aren't* made for you?

And when you do encounter those spaces, how often do you
find that those spaces have to *explain* to you *why* they're not
for you?

And if that's still troubling—let's talk about fragility.
And I'm not "calling anybody out" about anything.
I actually want to relate about some of my own fragility.

This one time I was hanging out with a friend of mine, who
is also a Hindu, and we were talking about religion . . .
Specifically my connection with religion—how important
it was for me to maintain my Hinduism—"It's my act of
resistance!"
And she said:
"Easy for you to say, you're a Brahmin."

And if you don't know what a Brahmin is—we're like the priests, and the knowledge keepers, philosophers . . .
. . . but we are also the *worst!* Like, currently, politcally, historically—we are the "highest caste"—if you buy that shit, which I don't. But rather than just acknowledging my goddamn caste privilege, my knee-jerk reaction was to say:

"You don't understand! You don't know what it was like in the Caribbean! You don't know how we had to fight to survive, when they wanted us to be erased!"

So that was a moment where I was fragile.
And there have been many.
And there will continue to be many.
So, if anyone here feels fragile about any of this . . .
That's totally cool.
Eventually that feeling burns out and we're all okay again.

These identities we use to divide ourselves are as much an illusion as a state border.
Now, on the one hand, we put these borders up to keep ouselves safe—because we are all potentially vulnerable when our conception of who we are is threatened.
But when we fail to recognize that they are in fact just that—an illusion—*Maya*—they become toxic, *poison.*

I want to show you all something.
Now that we're all together again.

    JIV gets a flambeau that was hidden somewhere on stage.

This is a flambeau.
And I know it looks like a Molotov cocktail—it's not.*
My dad used to always talk about this like it was the quint-
essential image for our people.
All over the village you'd see kids by the flambeau late at
night, doing their homework.
Just trying to learn.

He lights the flambeau.

This one time I was in Trinidad, and I was hanging out with
my little cousin, who's grown up around all this Hindu stuff
her whole life—and who was a teenager at the time and was
like soooooo over it!
And she said: "Do you really believe all this Hindu stuff?"
The ocean of milk? . . .
Cows are holy? . . .
We are all Jiv? . . .

And I said: "I choose to believe it."
I choose to believe it because I like what it does to my mind.
I like that I have to *challenge* myself to think beyond one
dimension of thinking.
The material dimension that we know how to describe.

He places the flambeau onto the altar.

---

* But, like, it really looks like a Molotov cocktail. It's basically an oil
lantern made of an old T-shirt and a glass bottle filled with oil.

Fire is a big part of Hinduism.
And for a lot of agrarian societies, like the tradition I
come from.

Fire is constantly creating and destroying all at the same
time . . .
It creates Maya, the illusion by showing us light and dark . . .

*He runs his hands through the flame, blackening the
white part of his hand.*

. . . and it destroys Maya because—as it lives—it eats everything around it.

He picks up a diya.

And in the end, it all turns to ash . . . just like the rest of us.

He lights the diya.

It's alive. It's pure life. That's why it dances like this . . .

If we're too distracted by the light, and can't see how the
dark is part of the same thing . . . then we give into Maya
. . . the illusion . . . The poison.

He picks up the milk and holds the lit diya.

And hey, man,
It's not easy to overcome Maya.
It's not so easy to overcome difference.
But you have to take the poison first if you wanna get the
Amrita ... if you wanna "take d milk."

> *He comes downstage, close to the audience with the
> milk and diya.*

You know why I think cows are awesome?

Because cows are my family.
And I like to think that you are my family too.

Do I really believe that?
... I don't know ... But I like what it does to my mind.

> *He triggers a final track* off the laptop. There are small
> lights evoking individual stars, or souls, or Jivas. He per-
> forms aarti for the audience as family. He kneels, bows
> to the milk, touching it to his forehead, and drinks from
> the bottle. He places the diya next to the milk bottle,
> stands, and as the music crescendos, he brings his hands
> together to acknowledge the audience. As the beat drops
> the Yantra is momentarily fully illuminated—the only
> source of light in addition to the live flame of the diya
> and the flambeau. The Yantra fades out to nothingness.*

> *End of play.*

---

* We used Apache Indian's "Om Namah Shivaya"—ideally whatever track
used would draw on a Shiva mantra.

Afterword

A lot has happened since we first premiered this project.

A lot is still to happen.

We are again at a moment in which the impacts of colonization, enslavement, and systemic oppression reverberate through our bodies. Breaking hearts and spirits . . . while fuelling others.

It never went away. And it never will.

If I believe one thing, it is that the future lies in affinity. Not just amongst those with shared experiences.

(Though that's a soothing balm in the interim . . .)

But in building affinity through the collision of difference. It is the difference of experience that will propel us to new ways of imagination.

The answers of the future will not be found in the past. Though unearthing hastily buried knowledge is fruitful.

Be it colonial histories or ancestral—we cannot rely on the best-written intentions of our ancestors. All the world's travesties have been born from good intentions. From a certain point of view.

And while I'd love to end with a joke, I offer you with all earnestness that laughter is the way forward. That forever undefined nature of the comic. Through ridicule we unseat the (often unrequested) privilege of "good" ideas.

These days when I'm thinking about what I desire in a performance space, I keep coming back to this idea of Satsang. A gathering of the not good, but truthful.

And the truth of it all . . . is pretty humorous. In the grand scheme of things.

But it's hard. To see humour in the burning of villages, the murder of innocents, the death of millions . . .

I almost lost one of my aunties in between the time of starting work on this publication and writing this note to you today. My father's eldest sister, Auntie Mam, who helped raise him. And then, suddenly, we lost their youngest sister, my auntie Doodoo, who Mam had also helped raise.

As a human I do struggle to find the humour in the face of loss. But I do remember a saying from my auntie Mam—who I am so grateful to still have here in this world with me, who faced so much adversity but could summarize it so succinctly:

"How you going, Mam?"

"I Dey."

Ha!

Ya . . . We Dey.

Jivesh Parasram
February 2021
Unceded Coast Salish Territories
(Vancouver, BC)

Acknowledgements

Take d Milk, Nah? was created iteratively over several years by Pandemic Theatre with its beginnings via Pressgang Theatre. It began to take its shape at b current performing arts's rock. paper.sistahz festival.

It development was supported by the Toronto Arts Council, the Ontario Arts Council, and the Canada Council for the Arts. Early development was seeded through the Ontario Arts Council Theatre Creators Reserve Program through Obsidian Theatre and Cahoots Theatre. An early version of what would become the play was driven by a presentation commitment from the Monsoon Festival and the RUTAS Festival. The production was the result of a presentation commitment by b current performing arts.

The publication would not be possible without the belief and commitment from Playwrights Canada Press—a commitment they made before understanding my loose definition of the word "deadline."

Much of the theoretical backing for this project is rooted deeply in the writing of Afro-pessimists and critical race scholars, particularly from a time in which scholarship and active participation in resistance held little to no separation. Frantz Fanon, W.E.B. Du Bois, and Aimé Césaire in particular.

I remain eternally grateful to the support of Catherine Hernandez at b current performing arts, as well as Andy

McKim and Régine Cadet at Theatre Passe Muraille for their belief in the scope of the project—beyond what we at Pandemic Theatre had considered. And to Aluna Theatre (RUTAS Festival) for their inclusion of Caribbean content in their broader programming of the Americas.

The project could not have existed were it not for the inspiration in form and content from two close friends and collaborators—Donna-Michelle St. Bernard and Adam Lazarus. Great acknowledgement is due to Guillermo Verdecchia, who introduced me to the form of augmented lecture, and who has—willingly or not—remained the closest thing to a mentor that I have in the realm of theatre.

The continued life of the premiere production was immensely supported by my colleagues at Rumble Theatre, Christie Watson and Kellee Ngan, as well as through the support of Chelsea Haberlin and Marcus Youssef at Neworld Theatre, and Heather Redfern at the Cultch.

The commitment to the continued life of this project owes special acknowledgement to Shanae Sodhi, who reminded me of its impact.

I would not have been able to complete this project were it not for the emotional support of my partner, Christine Quintana.

Finally, this project could not have happened, nor would it be the same, without the contributions of the creative team, Heather Bellingham, Anahita Dehbonehie, and Rebecca Vandevelde, and of course the contributions of Tom Arthur Davis and Graham Isador, my brothers, who believed in the project long before me.

Every action I have made in theatre and performance, and every opportunity to create work is due to the support of my family. I will love them until there is no love left in the cosmos.

Jivesh Parasram is an award-winning multidisciplinary artist of Indo Caribbean descent (Cairi/Trinidad & Tobago). Jivesh grew up in Mi'Kma'Ki (Nova Scotia) before moving to Tkoronto (Toronto). In 2009 he co-founded Pandemic Theatre, through which much of his work has been created, often in close collaboration with co-founder Tom Arthur Davis. He is a recipient of two Harold Awards for his service to the independent theatre community in Tkoronto, including the Ken McDougall Award. Jivesh won the 2018 Toronto Arts Foundation Emerging Artist Award, and was a member of the second cohort of the Cultural Leaders Lab with the Toronto Arts Council and the Banff Centre. In 2018, Jivesh took on the position of artistic director for Rumble Theatre. He lives primarily in the unceded Coast Salish territories (Vancouver, BC).

First edition: April 2021
Printed and bound in Canada by Rapido Books, Montreal

Jacket design by Jivesh Parasram
Author photo © Graham Isador

PLAYWRIGHTS
CANADA PRESS

202-269 Richmond St. w.
Toronto, ON
M5V 1X1

416.703.0013
info@playwrightscanada.com
www.playwrightscanada.com
@playcanpress